Robert Schultz

FUN with 5 FINGER JEWISH HOLIDAY SONGS

MW01485925

© 1992 Belwin Mills Publishing Corp. (ASCAP)
All Rights Assigned to and Controlled by Alfred Publishing Co., Inc.
All Rights Reserved including Public Performance. Printed in USA.

WARNING: Any duplication, adaptation or arrangement of the compositions contained in this collection, without the written consent of the owner, is an infringement of U.S. copyright law and subject to the penalties and liabilities provided therein.

PREFACE

The Fun With Five Finger Series is for the young, beginning piano student. It is designed to supplement any first year piano method.

This collection is organized in the order that the holidays occur throughout the year. Pieces appear in approximate order of difficulty within each holiday grouping. The arrangements are primarily melodies divided between the hands. A diagram of the keyboard appears at the beginning of each piece, showing the proper placement of the hands as the piece begins. Fingerings have been included throughout, but sparingly. The technical scope of the series includes the reading of rests, eighth notes, and an occasional dotted quarter note. Students will also occasionally encounter a brief hands-together passage or a simple pedal indication.

The goal of the Fun With Five Finger Series is to stimulate interest and enthusiasm in students. Every effort has been made to capture the beauty of the original melodies in a way that not only satisfies the younger student's desire to play familiar music, but satisfies the requirements of the teacher who insists on using accurate and pianistic arrangements which will correlate with and reinforce the teaching of standard technique and the classics.

Robert Schultz

L'SHANA TOVA

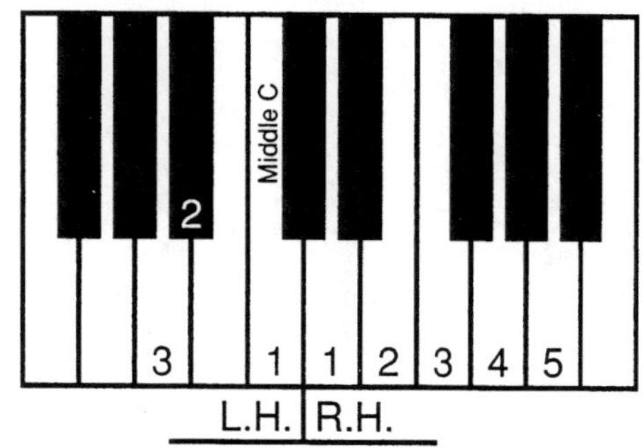
Middle C
2
3
1
1
2
3
4
5
L.H.
R.H.

TRADITIONAL
Arranged by ROBERT SCHULTZ

Slowly
1
L' - sha - na to - va ti - ka - tey - vu l' - sha -
mp
1

na to - va ti - ka - tey - vu ti - ka -

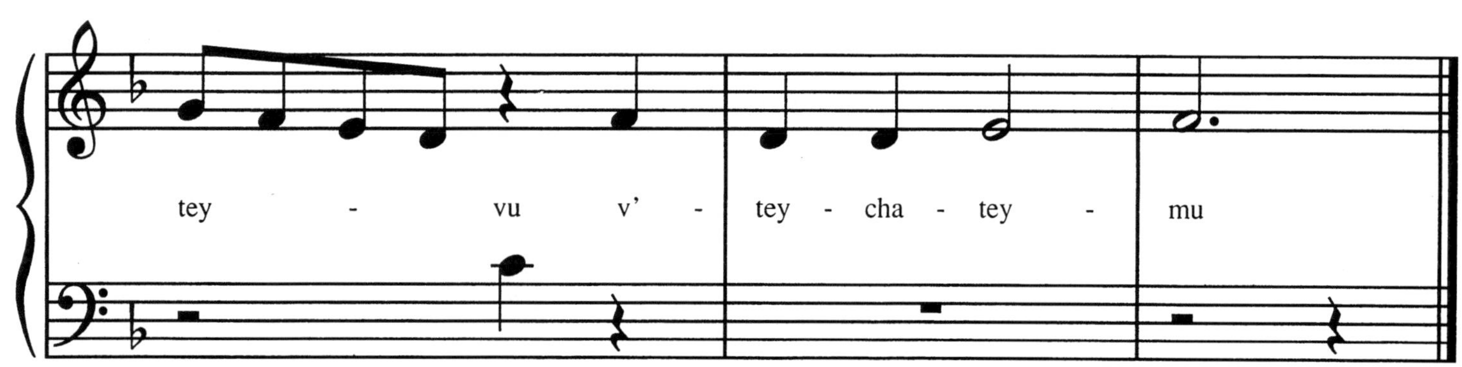
tey - vu v' - tey - cha - tey - mu

May you be inscribed for a good year.

© 1992 by BEAM ME UP MUSIC, c/o Belwin Mills Publishing Corp. (ASCAP)
All Rights Assigned to and Controlled by Alfred Publishing Co., Inc.
All Rights Reserved including Public Performance. Printed in USA.

TAPUCHIM UD'VASH

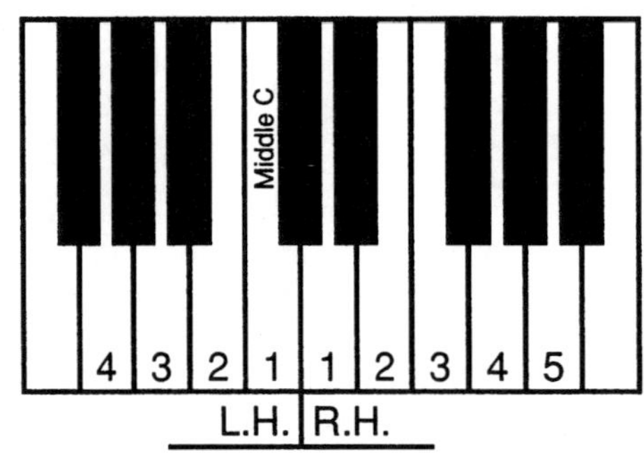
Middle C
4 3 2 1 1 2 3 4 5
L.H. R.H.

TRADITIONAL
Arranged by ROBERT SCHULTZ

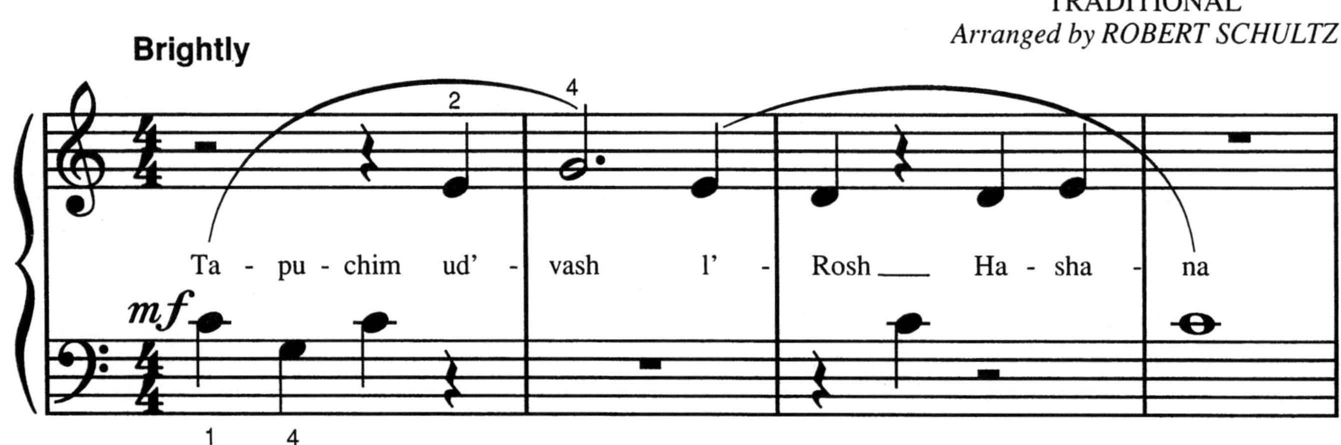
Brightly
2
4
Ta - pu - chim ud' - vash l' - Rosh Ha - sha - na
mf
1 4

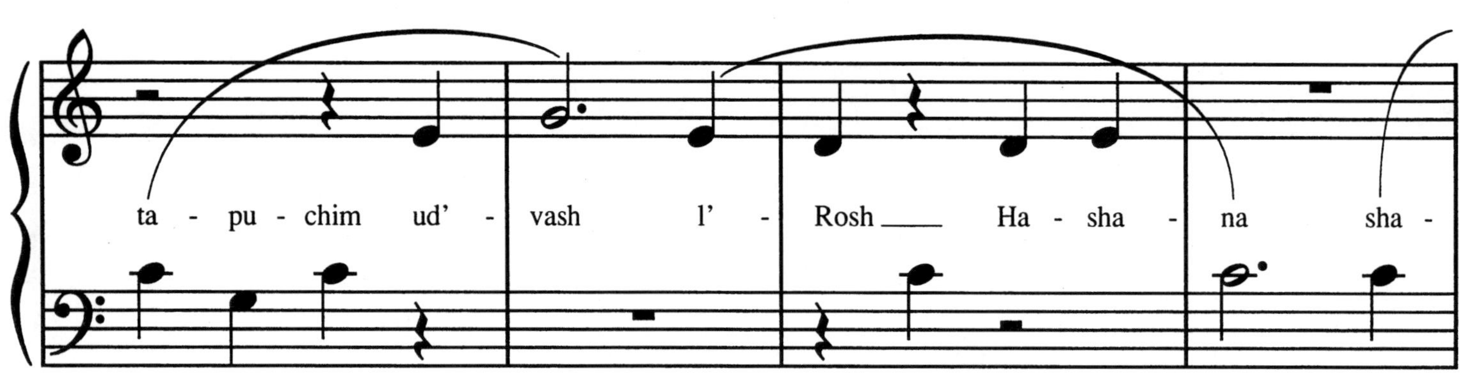
ta - pu - chim ud' - vash l' - Rosh Ha - sha - na sha -

5
na to - va sha - na m' - tu - ka sha -

© 1992 by BEAM ME UP MUSIC, c/o Belwin Mills Publishing Corp. (ASCAP)
All Rights Assigned to and Controlled by Alfred Publishing Co., Inc.
All Rights Reserved including Public Performance. Printed in USA.

na to - va sha - na m' - tu - ka

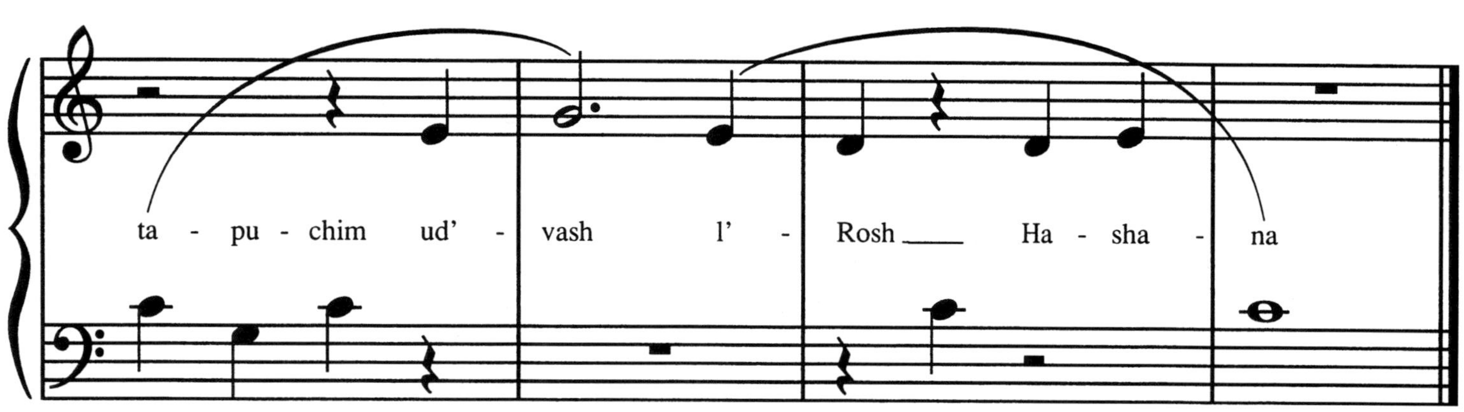
ta - pu - chim ud' - vash l' - Rosh Ha - sha - na

Apples dipped in honey for Rosh Hashana,
Apples dipped in honey for Rosh Hashana;
A good new year, a sweet new year,
A good new year, a sweet new year;
Apples dipped in honey for Rosh Hashana.

LET'S BE FRIENDS

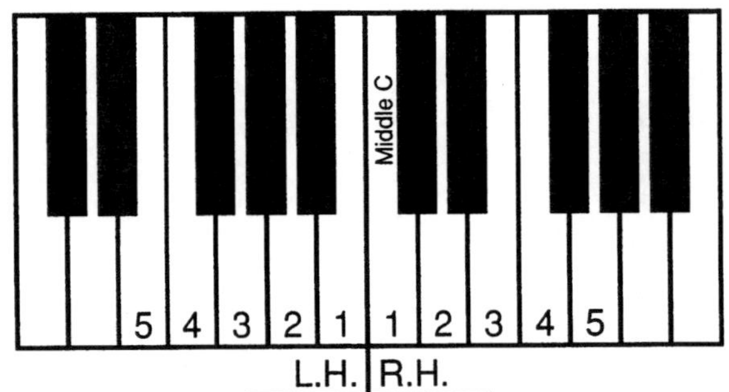
Middle C
5 4 3 2 1 1 2 3 4 5
L.H. R.H.

TRADITIONAL
Arranged by ROBERT SCHULTZ

Moderately

1
mf
Let's be friends, make a - mends, now's the time to say I'm sor - ry.
5 2

Fine
1
Let's be friends, make a - mends, please say you'll for - give me.

The ten days of T'-shu - va, time to make up, time to pray.

D.C. al Fine
Take my hand and I'll take yours, let's be friends for al - ways.

© 1992 by BEAM ME UP MUSIC, c/o Belwin Mills Publishing Corp. (ASCAP)
All Rights Assigned to and Controlled by Alfred Publishing Co., Inc.
All Rights Reserved including Public Performance. Printed in USA.

CHANUKAH

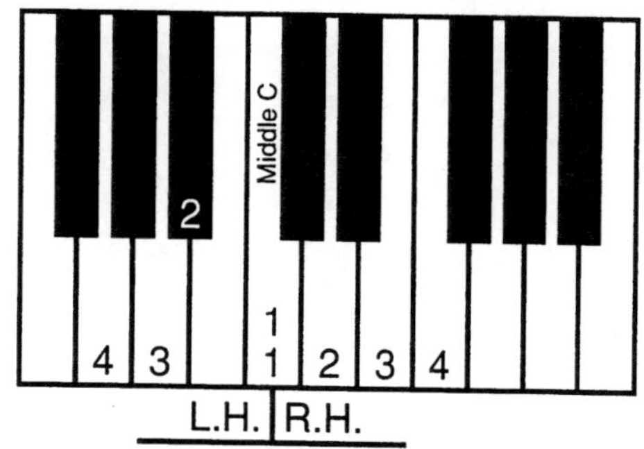
Middle C
2
1
4 3 1 2 3 4
L.H. R.H.

TRADITIONAL
Arranged by ROBERT SCHULTZ

With spirit

4
mf
Cha - nu - kah Cha - nu - kah chag ya - fe kol kach
1

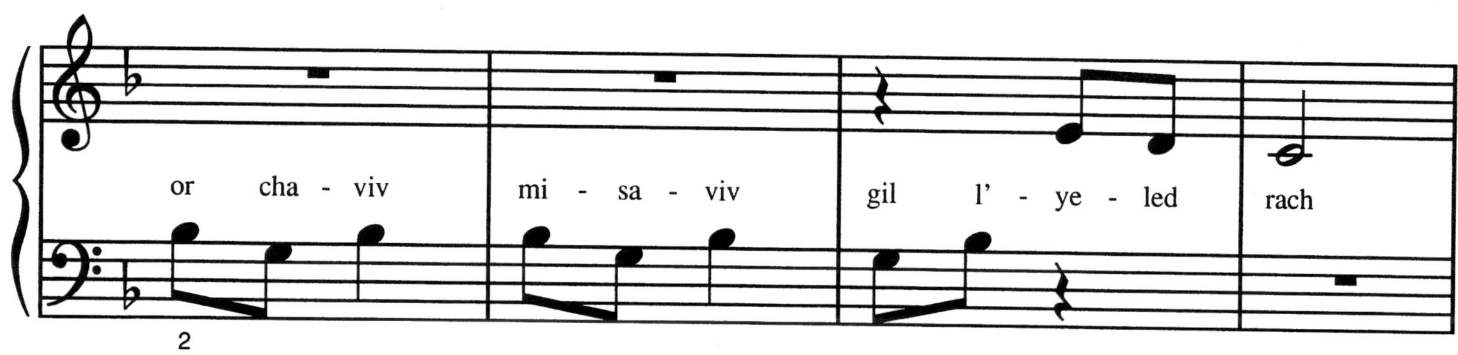
or cha - viv mi - sa - viv gil l' - ye - led rach
2

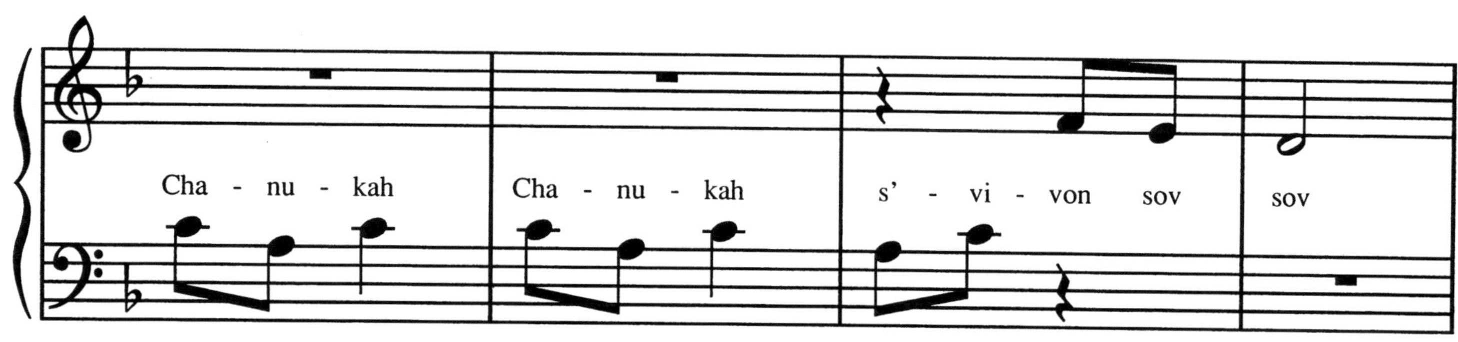
Cha - nu - kah Cha - nu - kah s' - vi - von sov sov

sov sov sov sov sov sov ma na - im va - tov

© 1992 by BEAM ME UP MUSIC, c/o Belwin Mills Publishing Corp. (ASCAP)
All Rights Assigned to and Controlled by Alfred Publishing Co., Inc.
All Rights Reserved including Public Performance. Printed in USA.

I HAVE A LITTLE DREYDL

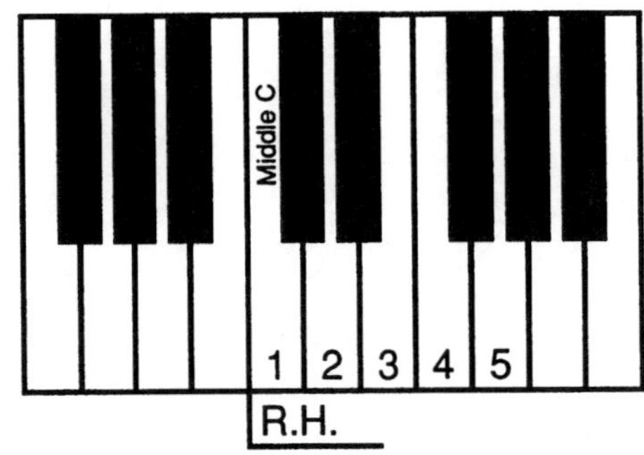
Middle C
1 2 3 4 5
R.H.

S.E. GOLDFARB
Arranged by ROBERT SCHULTZ

Playfully
5
1
I have a lit - tle drey - dl, I made it out of clay and
mf

Chorus:
when it's dry and read - y, then drey - dl I shall play. Oh

drey - dl, drey - dl, drey - dl, I made it out of clay; oh

© 1992 by BEAM ME UP MUSIC, c/o Belwin Mills Publishing Corp. (ASCAP)
All Rights Assigned to and Controlled by Alfred Publishing Co., Inc.
All Rights Reserved including Public Performance. Printed in USA.

drey - dl, drey - dl,
drey - dl, now
drey - dl I shall
play.

Verse 2:
It has a lovely body,
With leg so short and thin
And when it is all tired,
It drops and then I win.
(Chorus:)

Verse 3:
My dreydl's always playful,
It loves to dance and spin;
A happy game of dreydl,
Come play, now, let's begin.
(Chorus:)

S'VIVON

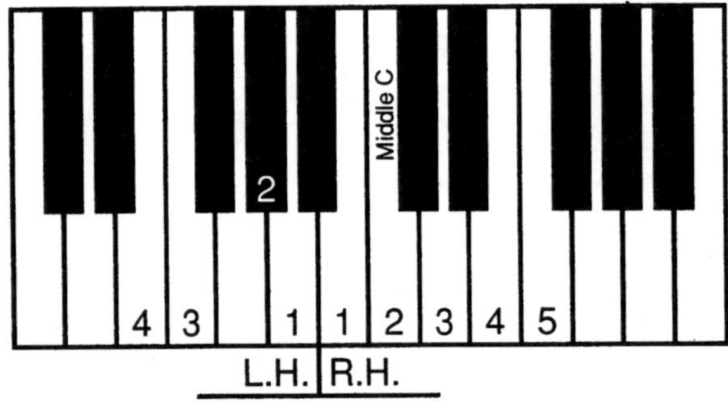
Middle C
2
4 3 1 1 2 3 4 5
L.H. R.H.

Words by L. KIPNIS
TRADITIONAL FOLK SONG
Arranged by ROBERT SCHULTZ

With spirit

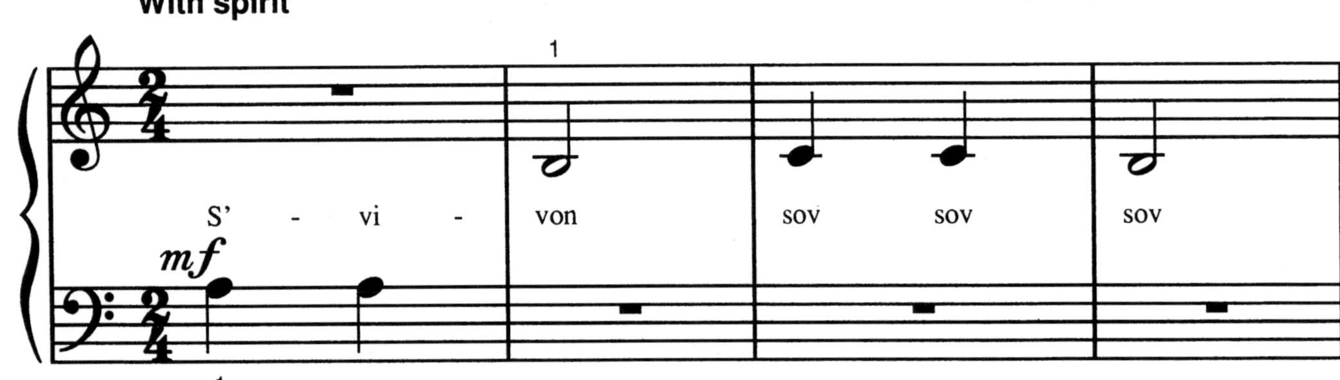
1
S' - vi - von sov sov sov
mf
1

Cha - nu - kah hu chag tov

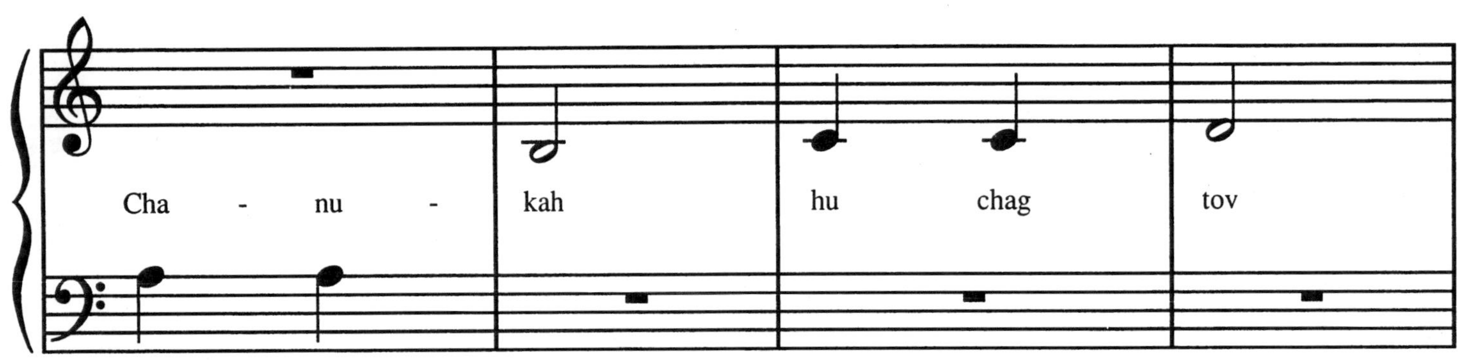
Cha - nu - kah hu chag tov

© 1992 by BEAM ME UP MUSIC, c/o Belwin Mills Publishing Corp. (ASCAP)
All Rights Assigned to and Controlled by Alfred Publishing Co., Inc.
All Rights Reserved including Public Performance. Printed in USA.

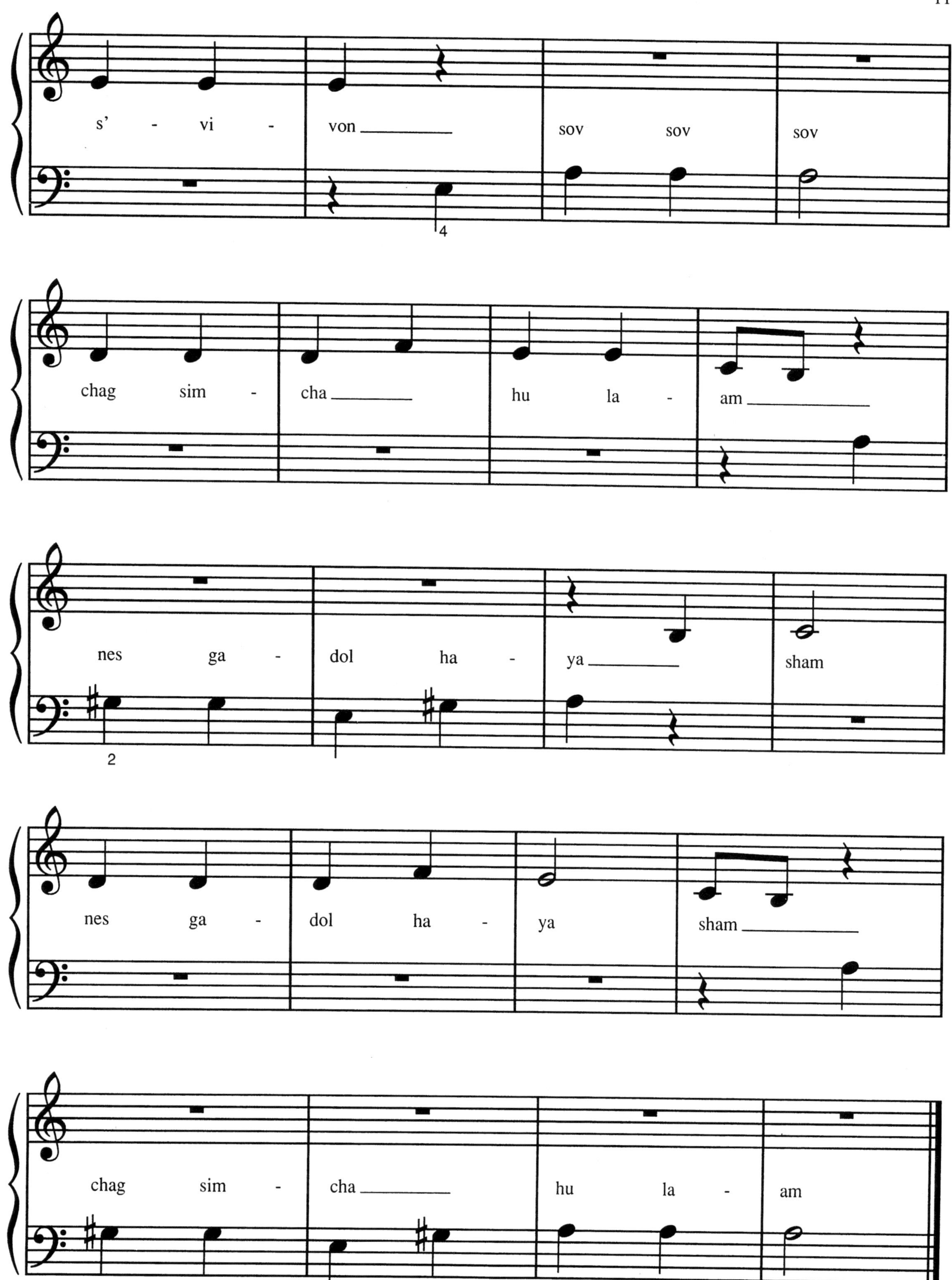
s' - vi - von sov sov sov
chag sim - cha hu la - am
nes ga - dol ha - ya sham
nes ga - dol ha - ya sham
chag sim - cha hu la - am
4
2

Y'MEY HACHANUKAH

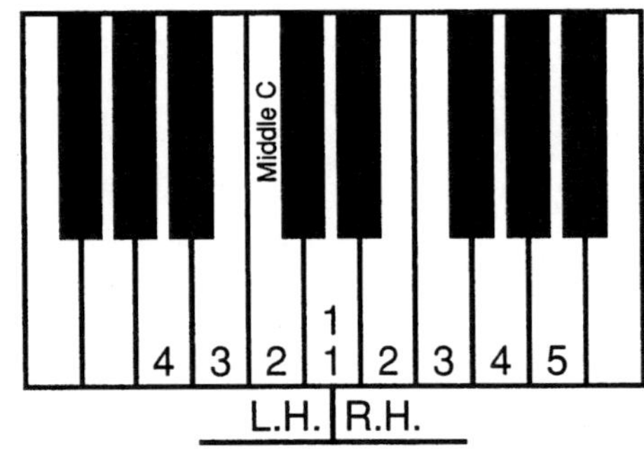
Middle C
4 3 2 1 1 2 3 4 5
L.H. R.H.

Words by A. EVRONIN
TRADITIONAL FOLK SONG
Arranged by ROBERT SCHULTZ

Moderately
mf
2
4
1
Y' - mey ha - Cha - nu - kah Cha - nu - kat mik - da - shey nu b' -

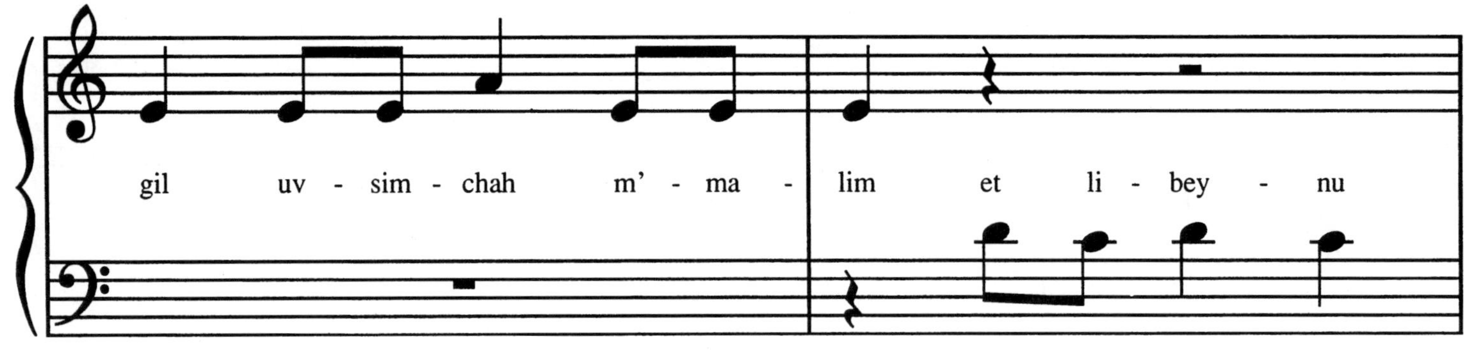
gil uv - sim - chah m' - ma - lim et li - bey - nu

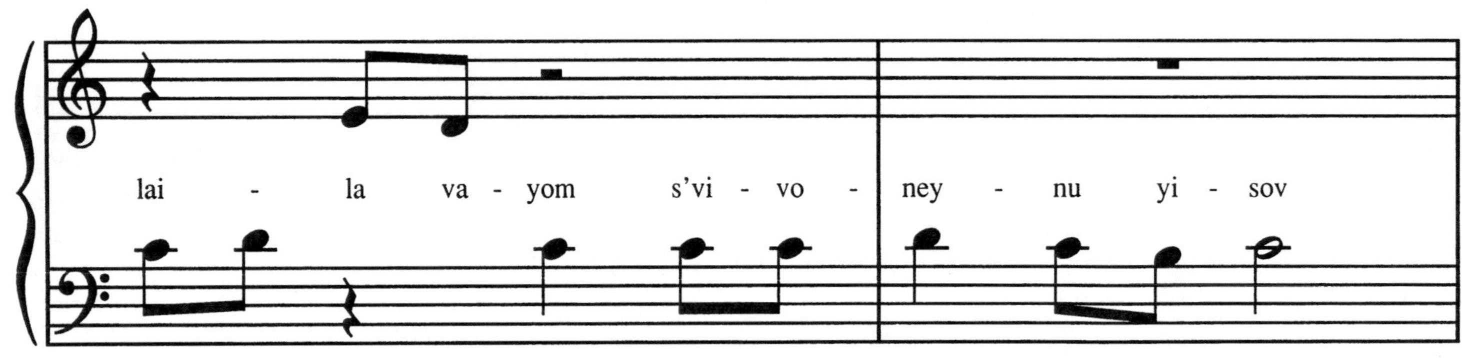
lai - la va - yom s'vi - vo - ney - nu yi - sov

© 1992 by BEAM ME UP MUSIC, c/o Belwin Mills Publishing Corp. (ASCAP)
All Rights Assigned to and Controlled by Alfred Publishing Co., Inc.
All Rights Reserved including Public Performance. Printed in USA.

suf - ga - ni - yot no - chal bam la - rov ha -
i - ru had - li - ku ne - rot Cha - nu - kah ra - bim
al ha - ni - sim v' - al ha - nif - la - ot a -
sher chol - l' - lu ha - ma - ka - bim al ha - ni - sim v' -
al ha - nif - la - ot a - sher chol - l' - lu ha - ma - ka - bim

LICHVOD HACHANUKAH

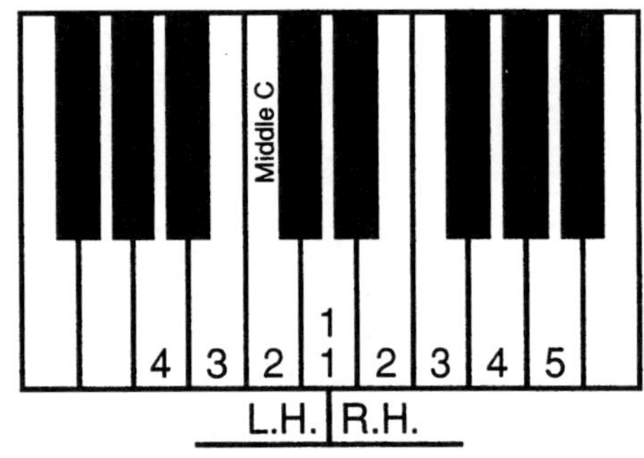
Middle C
4 3 2 1
1 2 3 4 5
L.H. R.H.

TRADITIONAL FOLK SONG
Arranged by ROBERT SCHULTZ

Moderately

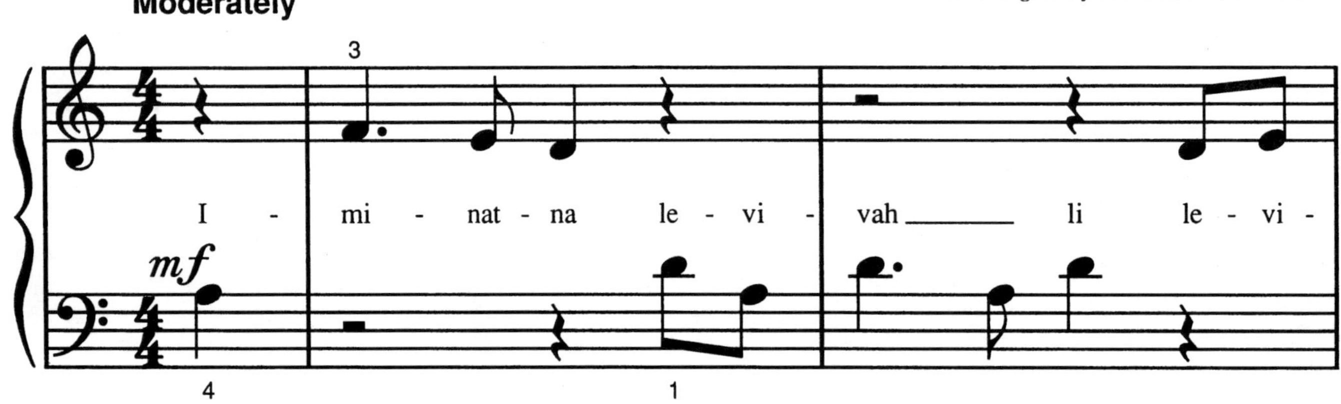
3
I - mi - nat - na le - vi - vah li le - vi -
mf
4
1

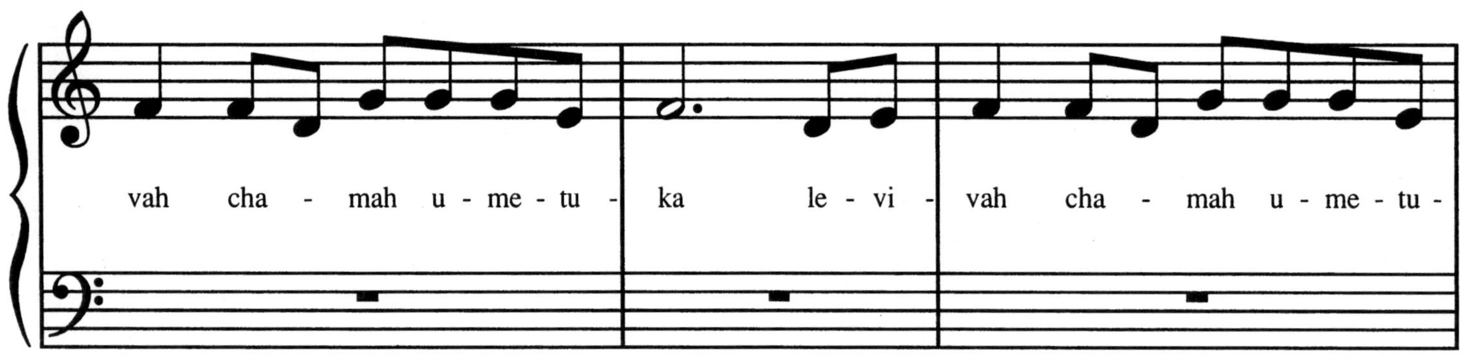
vah cha - mah u - me - tu - ka le - vi - vah cha - mah u - me - tu -

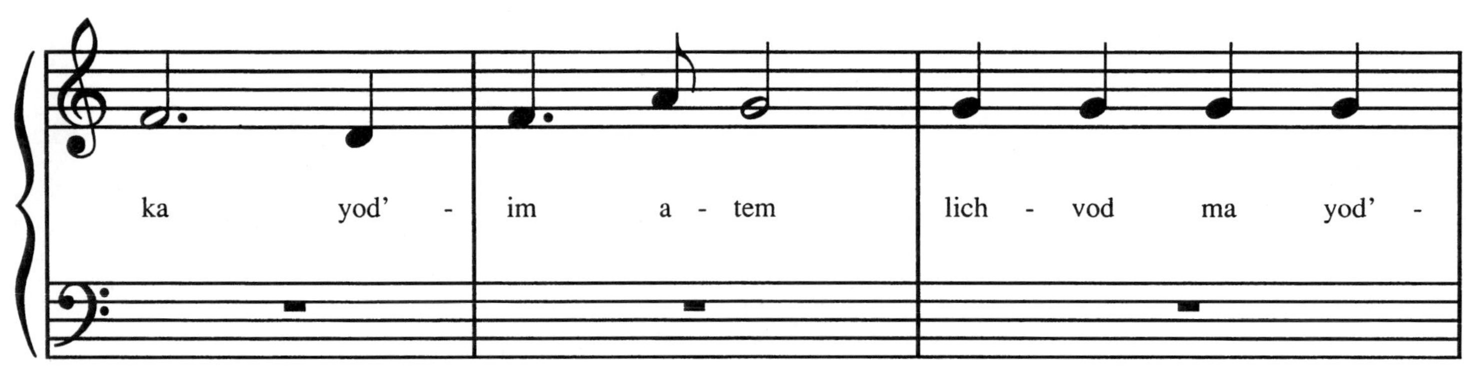
ka yod' - im a - tem lich - vod ma yod' -

© 1992 by BEAM ME UP MUSIC, c/o Belwin Mills Publishing Corp. (ASCAP)
All Rights Assigned to and Controlled by Alfred Publishing Co., Inc.
All Rights Reserved including Public Performance. Printed in USA.

im a - tem
lich - vod ma yod' -
im a - tem

lich - vod ma lich -
vod ha - Cha - nu -
kah

Verse 2:
A-vi hid-lik nerot li
Ve-sha-mash lo a-vou-ka
Ve-sha-mash lo a-vou-ka
Yod'im atem lich-vod mah
Yod'im atem lich-vod mah
Yod'im atem lich-vod mah
Lich-vod ha-Chanukah

BARUCH SHEL CHANUKAH

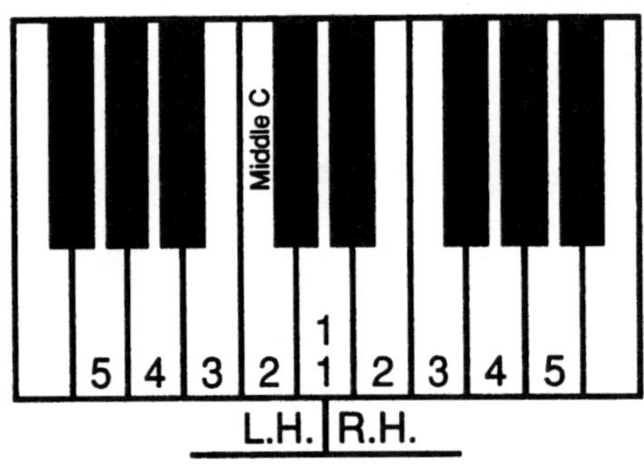
Middle C
5 4 3 2 1 1 2 3 4 5
L.H. R.H.

TRADITIONAL
Arranged by ROBERT SCHULTZ

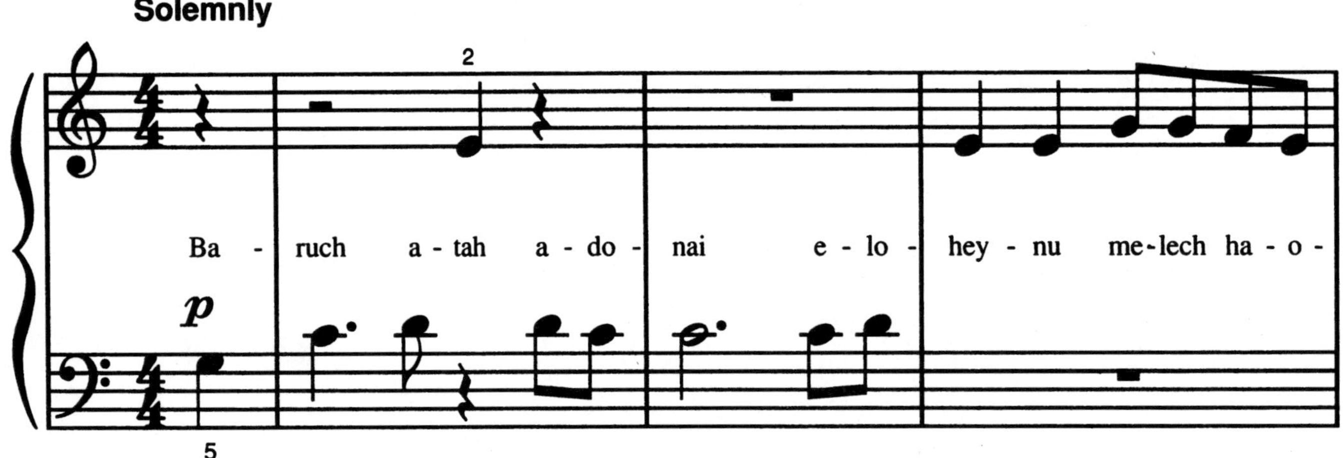
Solemnly
2
Ba - ruch a - tah a - do - nai e - lo - hey - nu me-lech ha - o -
p
5

lam a - sher kid - sha - nu b' - mitz - vo - tav v' - tsi -
she - a - sa - ni - sim la - vo - tey - nu ba - ya -

© 1992 by BEAM ME UP MUSIC, c/o Belwin Mills Publishing Corp. (ASCAP)
All Rights Assigned to and Controlled by Alfred Publishing Co., Inc.
All Rights Reserved including Public Performance. Printed in USA.

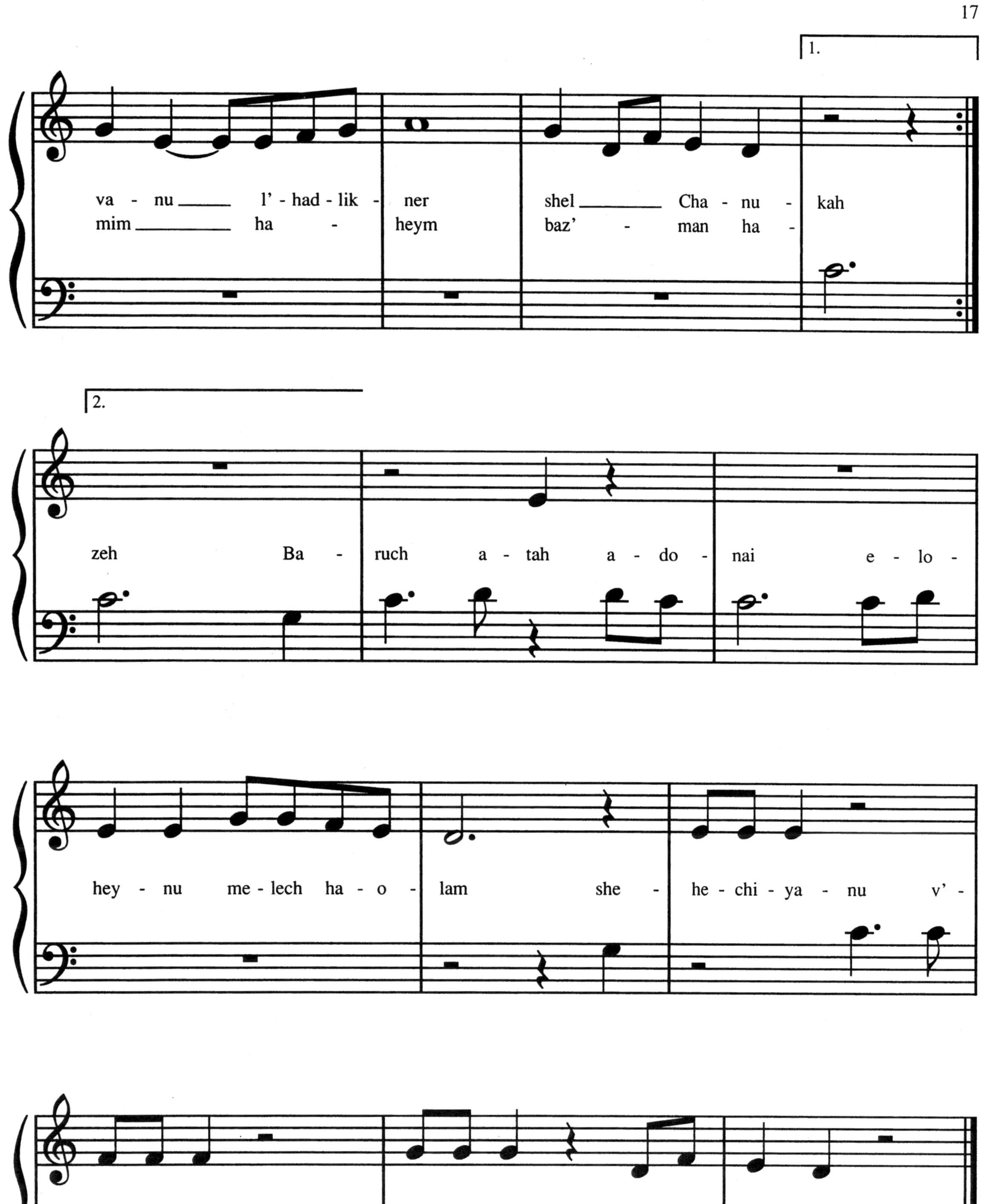
1.
va - nu l' - had - lik - ner shel Cha - nu - kah
mim ha - heym baz' - man ha -
2.
zeh Ba - ruch a - tah a - do - nai e - lo -
hey - nu me - lech ha - o - lam she - he - chi - ya - nu v' -
ki - y' - ma - nu v' - hi - gi - a - nu laz' - man ha - zeh
rit.

MAOZ TZUR
(Rock of Ages)

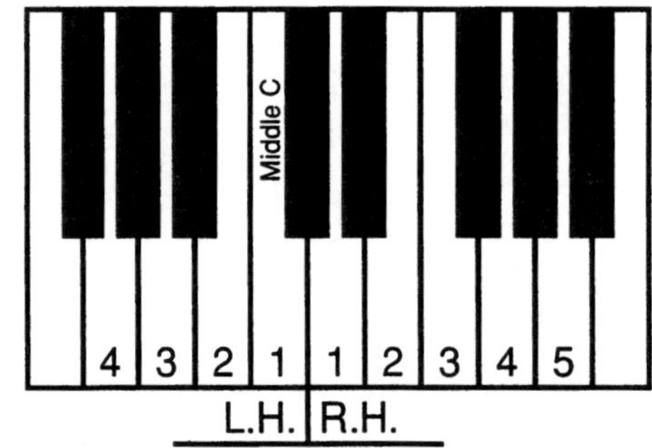
Middle C
4 3 2 1 1 2 3 4 5
L.H. R.H.

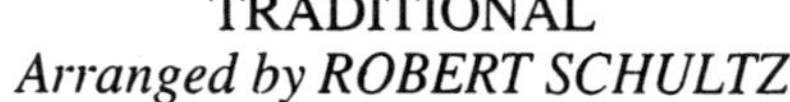
TRADITIONAL
Arranged by ROBERT SCHULTZ

Majestically

3
4
Ma - oz tzur y' - shu - a - ti l' - cha na - e l'-sha - bey - ach
mf
1

ti - kon beyt t' - fi - la - ti v' - sham to - da n' - za bey - ach

2
4
l'et ta - chin mat - bey - ach mi - tzor ha - m'na - bey - ach

© 1992 by BEAM ME UP MUSIC, c/o Belwin Mills Publishing Corp. (ASCAP)
All Rights Assigned to and Controlled by Alfred Publishing Co., Inc.
All Rights Reserved including Public Performance. Printed in USA.

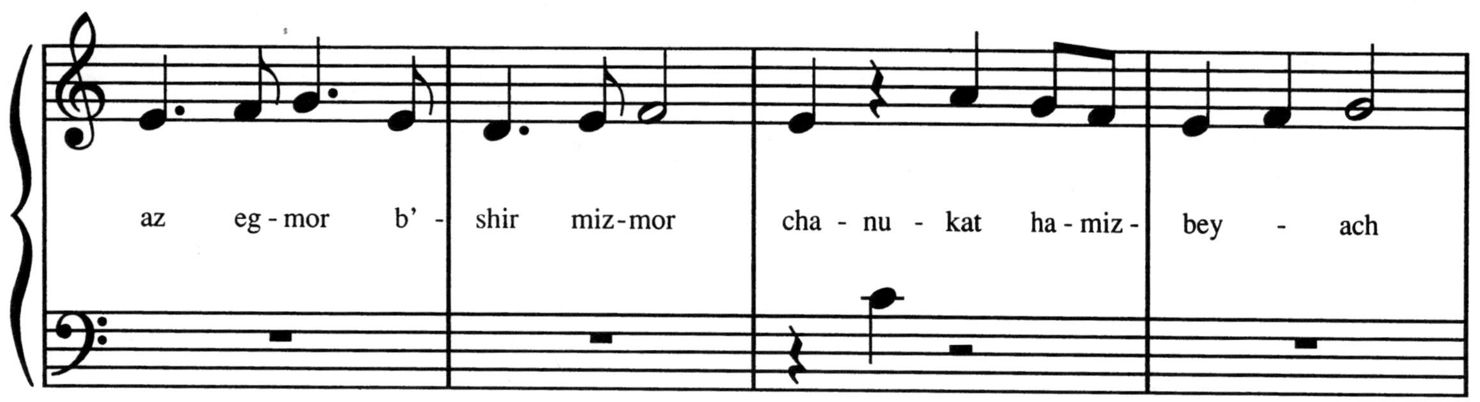
az eg - mor b' - shir miz-mor cha - nu - kat ha - miz - bey - ach

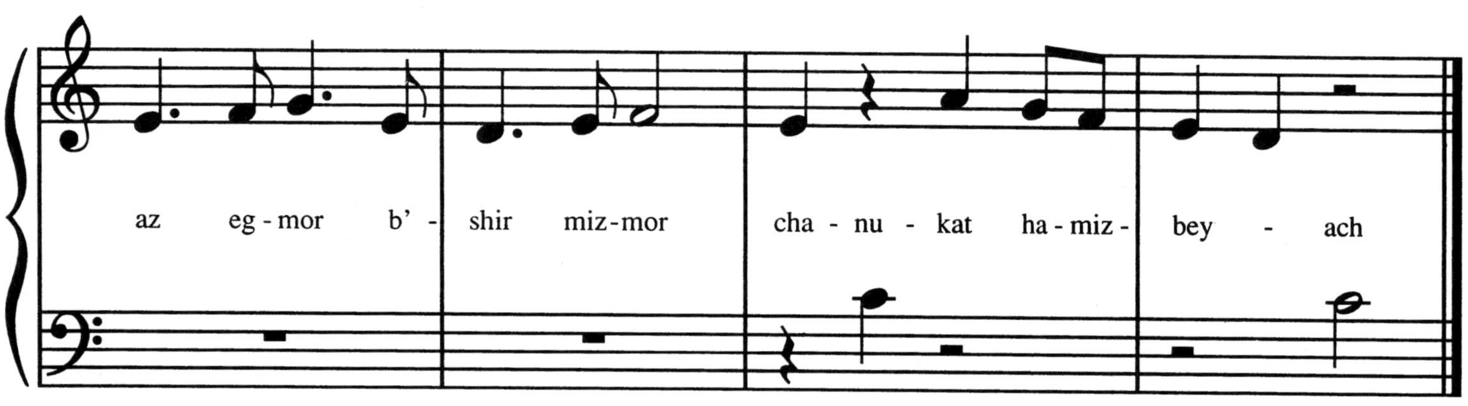
az eg - mor b' - shir miz-mor cha - nu - kat ha - miz - bey - ach

Rock of ages, let our song
Praise Thy saving power;
Thou, amidst the raging foes,
Wast our shelt'ring tower.
Furious, they assailed us,
But Thine arm availed us,
And Thy word broke their sword
When our own strength failed us.

HANEROT HALALU

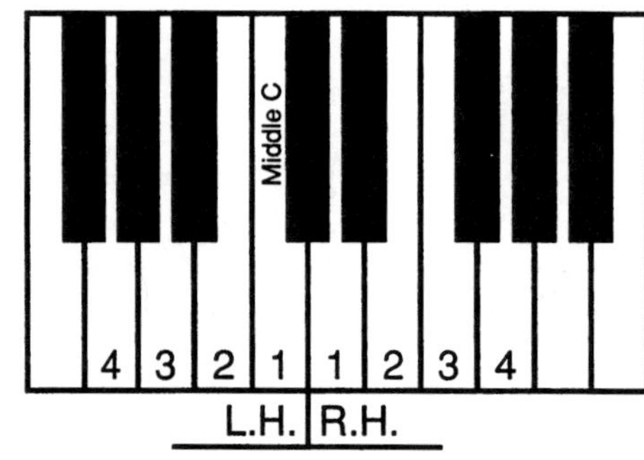
Middle C
4 3 2 1 1 2 3 4
L.H. R.H.

TRADITIONAL FOLK SONG
Arranged by ROBERT SCHULTZ

March tempo
Ha - ne - rot ha - la - lu she - a - nu mad - li - kin ha -
she - a - si - ta la - a - vo - tey - nu
f
4
2

1
ne - rot ha - la - lu she - a - nu mad - li - kin al ha - ni - sim v' -
she - a - si - ta la - a - vo - tey - nu ba - ya - mim ha - hem baz -
1

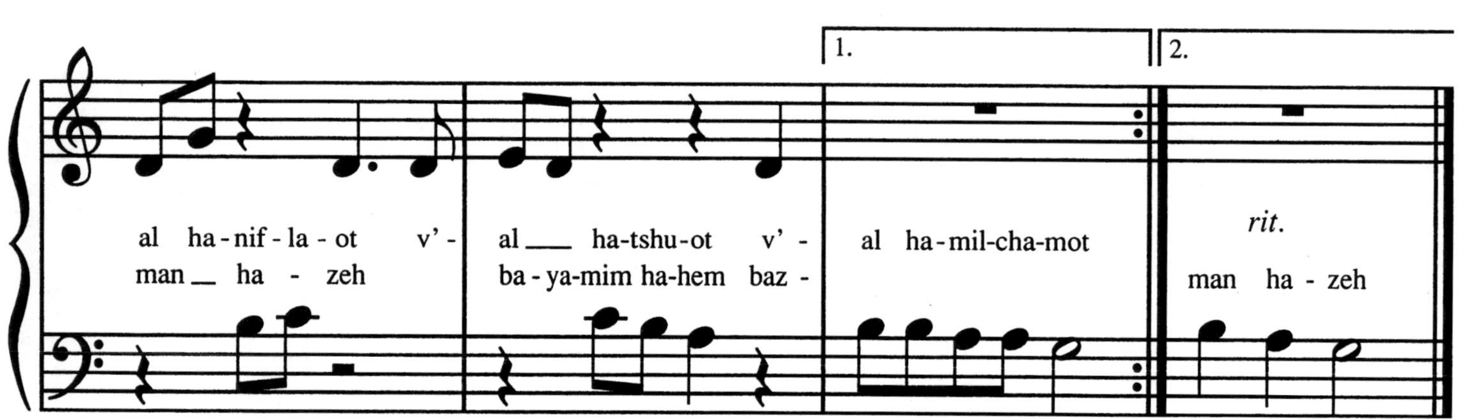
1.
2.
al ha - nif - la - ot v' - al ha - tshu - ot v' - al ha - mil - cha - mot
man ha - zeh ba - ya - mim ha - hem baz - man ha - zeh
rit.

© 1992 by BEAM ME UP MUSIC, c/o Belwin Mills Publishing Corp. (ASCAP)
All Rights Assigned to and Controlled by Alfred Publishing Co., Inc.
All Rights Reserved including Public Performance. Printed in USA.

CHAG PURIM

TRADITIONAL
Arranged by ROBERT SCHULTZ

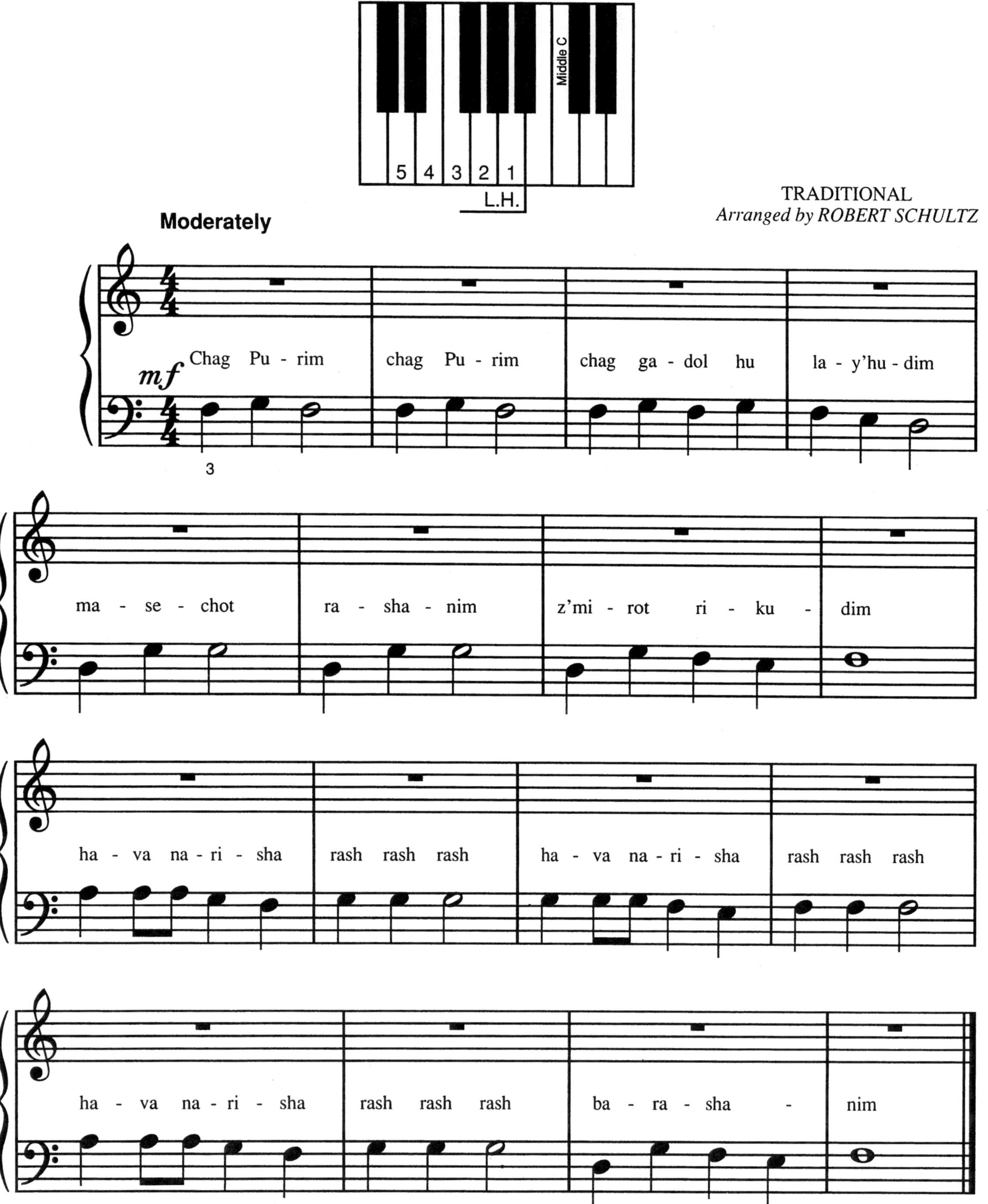

Middle C
5 4 3 2 1
L.H.
Moderately
mf
Chag Pu - rim
chag Pu - rim
chag ga - dol hu
la - y'hu - dim
3
ma - se - chot
ra - sha - nim
z'mi - rot ri - ku - dim
ha - va na - ri - sha
rash rash rash
ha - va na - ri - sha
rash rash rash
ha - va na - ri - sha
rash rash rash
ba - ra - sha - nim

© 1992 by BEAM ME UP MUSIC, c/o Belwin Mills Publishing Corp. (ASCAP)
All Rights Assigned to and Controlled by Alfred Publishing Co., Inc.
All Rights Reserved including Public Performance. Printed in USA.

DAYENU

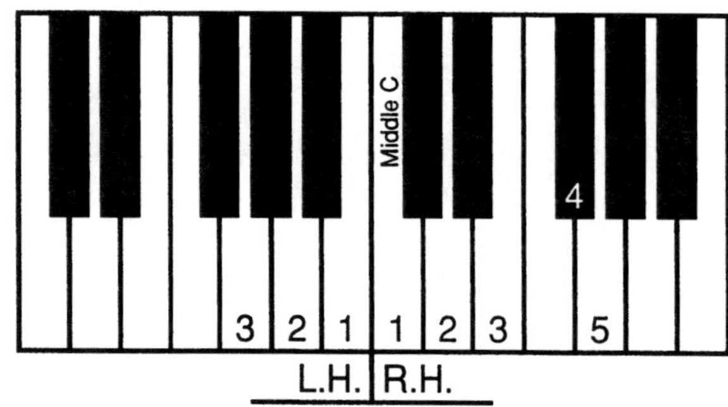
Middle C
4
3 2 1 1 2 3 5
L.H. R.H.

TRADITIONAL FOLK SONG
Arranged by ROBERT SCHULTZ

Brightly

2
I - lu ho - tzi ho - tzi - a - nu ho - tzi - a - nu mi - mitz - ra - yim
mf
1

ho - tzi - a - nu mi - mitz - ra - yim da - ye - nu

i - lu ho - tzi ho - tzi - a - nu ho - tzi - a - nu mi - mitz - ra - yim

© 1992 by BEAM ME UP MUSIC, c/o Belwin Mills Publishing Corp. (ASCAP)
All Rights Assigned to and Controlled by Alfred Publishing Co., Inc.
All Rights Reserved including Public Performance. Printed in USA.

ho - tzi - a - nu mi - mitz - ra - yim da - ye - nu
da - da - ye - nu da - da - ye - nu
5 4
da - da - ye - nu da - ye - nu da - ye - nu da - ye - nu
da - da - ye - nu da - da - ye - nu
da - da - ye - nu da - ye - nu da - ye - nu

ARTZA ALINU

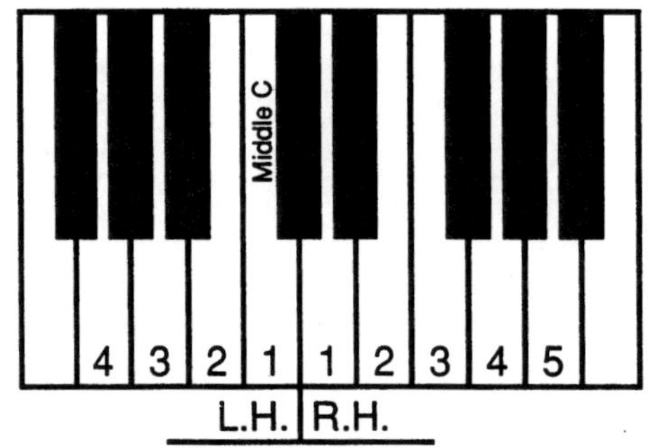
Middle C
4 3 2 1 1 2 3 4 5
L.H. R.H.

TRADITIONAL
Arranged by ROBERT SCHULTZ

March

2
1
Ar - tza a - li - nu ar - tza a - li - nu
mf
3
1

ar - tza a - li - nu

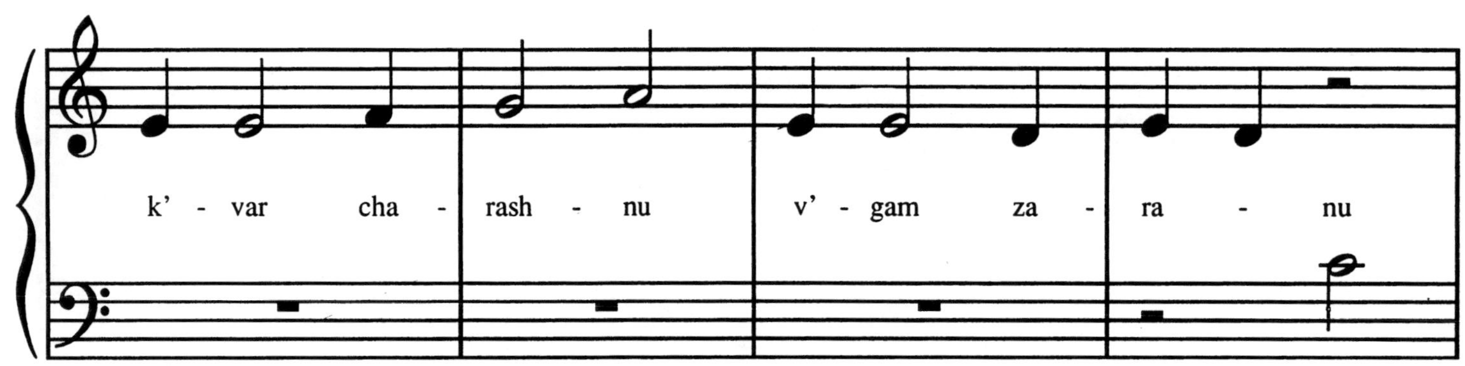
k' - var cha - rash - nu v' - gam za - ra - nu

© 1992 by BEAM ME UP MUSIC, c/o Belwin Mills Publishing Corp. (ASCAP)
All Rights Assigned to and Controlled by Alfred Publishing Co., Inc.
All Rights Reserved including Public Performance. Printed in USA.

k' - var cha - rash - nu v' - gam za - ra - nu
a - val od lo ka - tzar - nu
a - val od lo ka - tzar - nu
a - val od lo ka - tzar - nu
4
a - val od lo ka - tzar - nu

HATIKVA

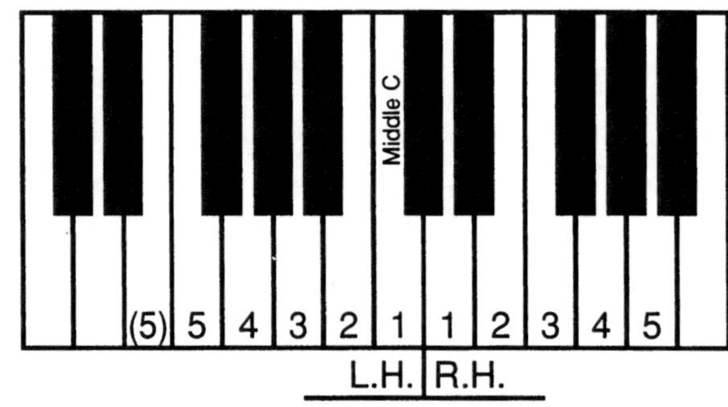
Middle C
(5) 5 4 3 2 1 1 2 3 4 5
L.H. R.H.

ISRAELI NATIONAL ANTHEM
Arranged by ROBERT SCHULTZ

Majestically
1
Kol od ba - ley - vav p' - ni - ma
mf
3

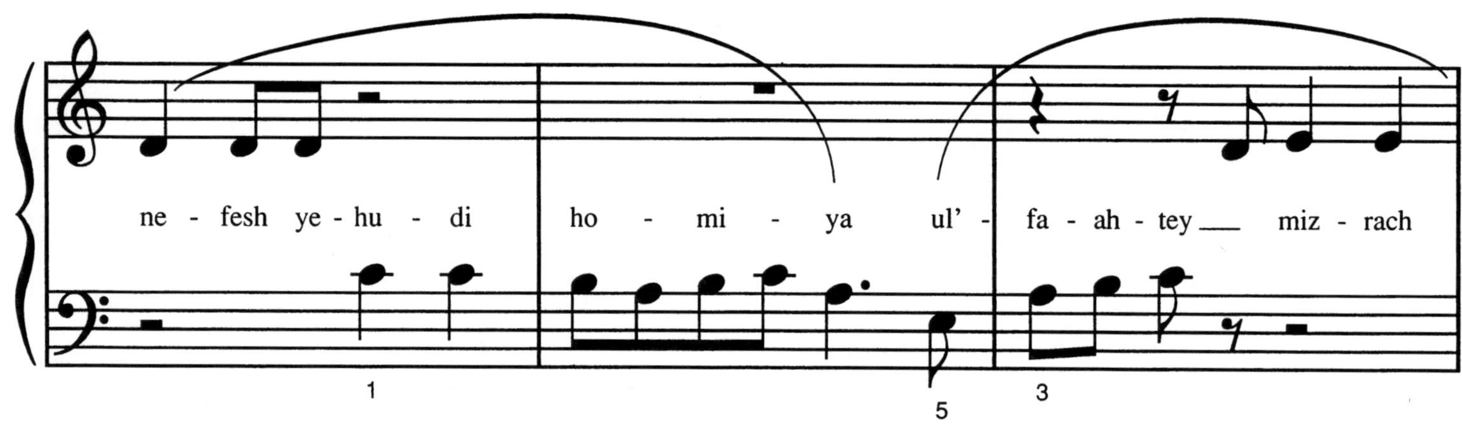
ne - fesh ye - hu - di ho - mi - ya ul' - fa - ah - tey miz - rach
1
5
3

kah - di - ma ah yin l' - Tzi - yon tzo - fi - ya

© 1992 by BEAM ME UP MUSIC, c/o Belwin Mills Publishing Corp. (ASCAP)
All Rights Assigned to and Controlled by Alfred Publishing Co., Inc.
All Rights Reserved including Public Performance. Printed in USA.

ohd lo av - da
tik - va - tey - nu
Ha - tik - va

shnoht al - pa - yim
lih - yoht ahm chuf - shi
b' - ahr - tzay - nu

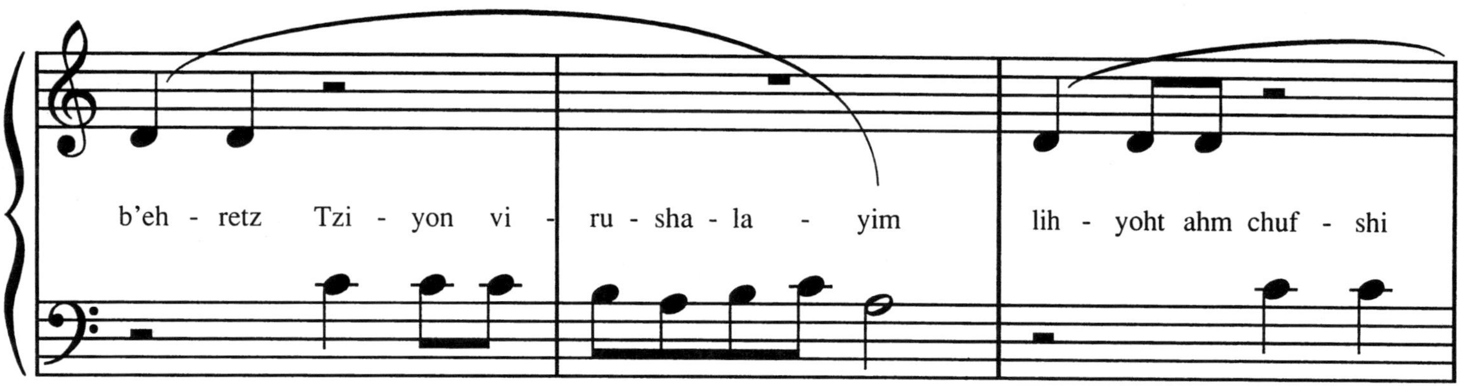
b'eh - retz Tzi - yon vi - ru - sha - la - yim
lih - yoht ahm chuf - shi

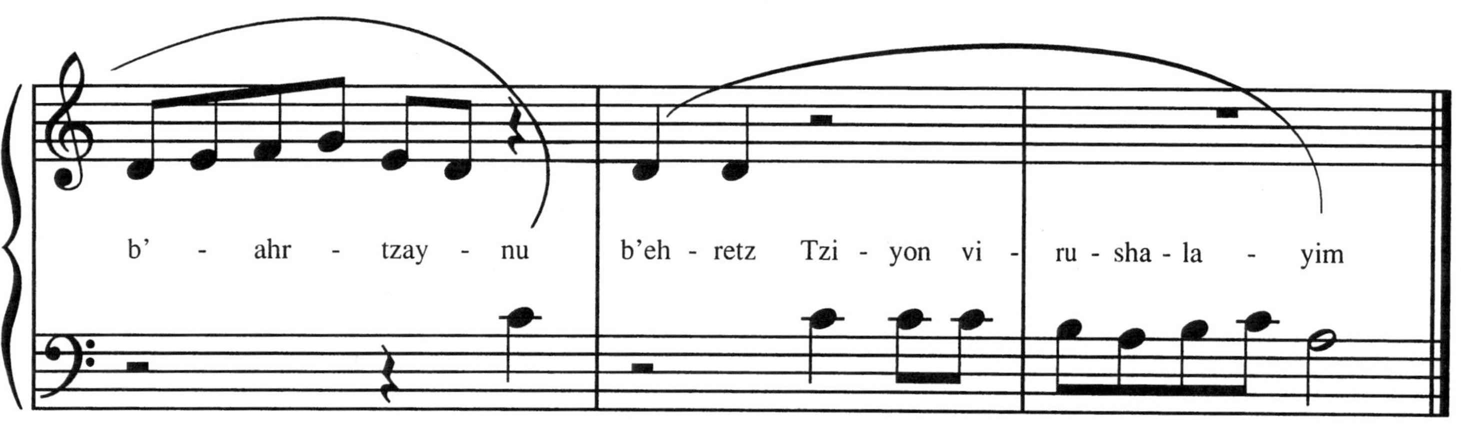
b' - ahr - tzay - nu
b'eh - retz Tzi - yon vi - ru - sha - la - yim

HAVA NAGILA

HASSIDIC
Arranged by ROBERT SCHULTZ

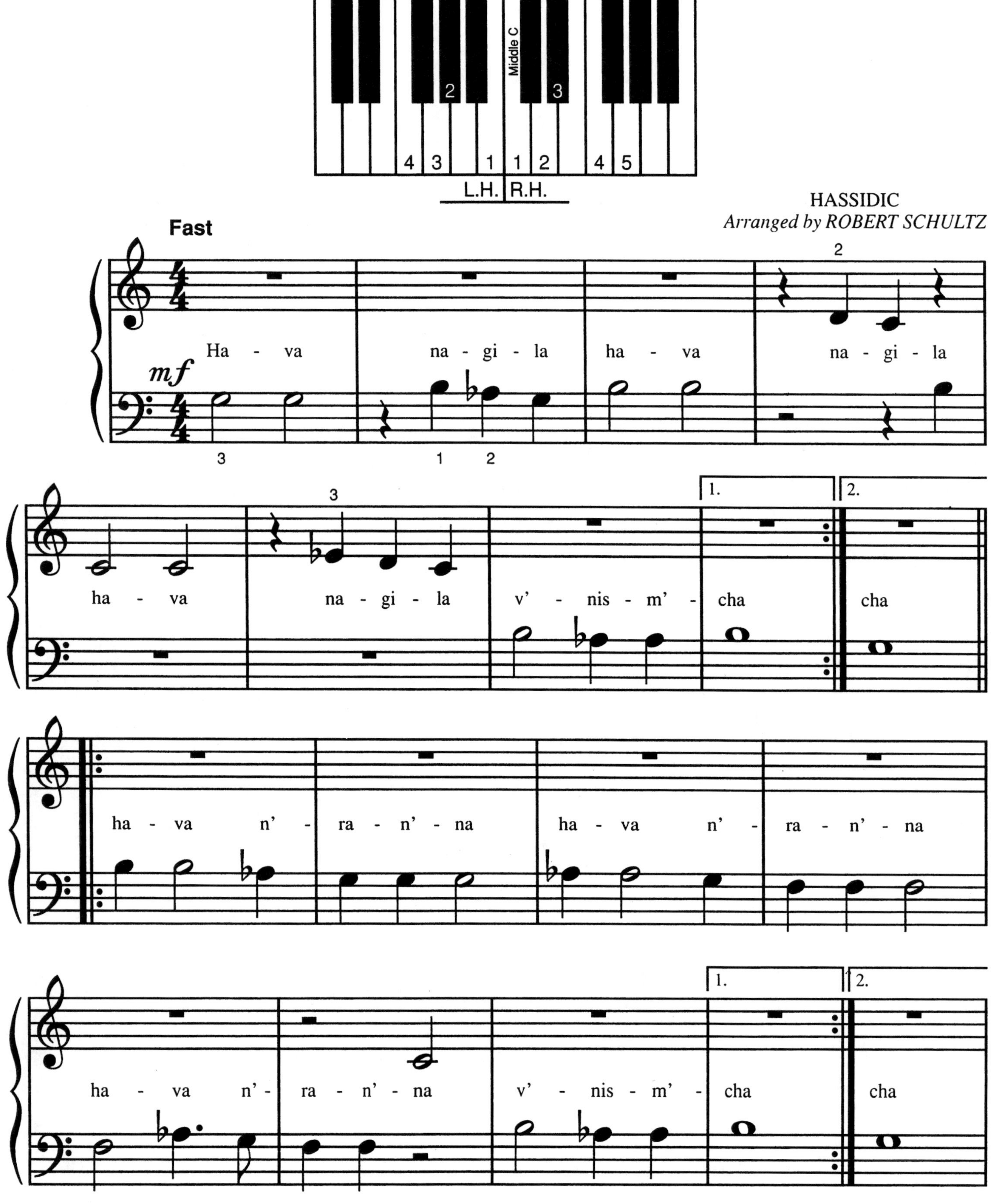
Middle C
L.H.
R.H.
Fast
mf
Ha - va na - gi - la ha - va na - gi - la
ha - va na - gi - la v' - nis - m' - cha cha
ha - va n' - ra - n' - na ha - va n' - ra - n' - na
ha - va n' - ra - n' - na v' - nis - m' - cha cha

© 1992 by BEAM ME UP MUSIC, c/o Belwin Mills Publishing Corp. (ASCAP)
All Rights Assigned to and Controlled by Alfred Publishing Co., Inc.
All Rights Reserved including Public Performance. Printed in USA.

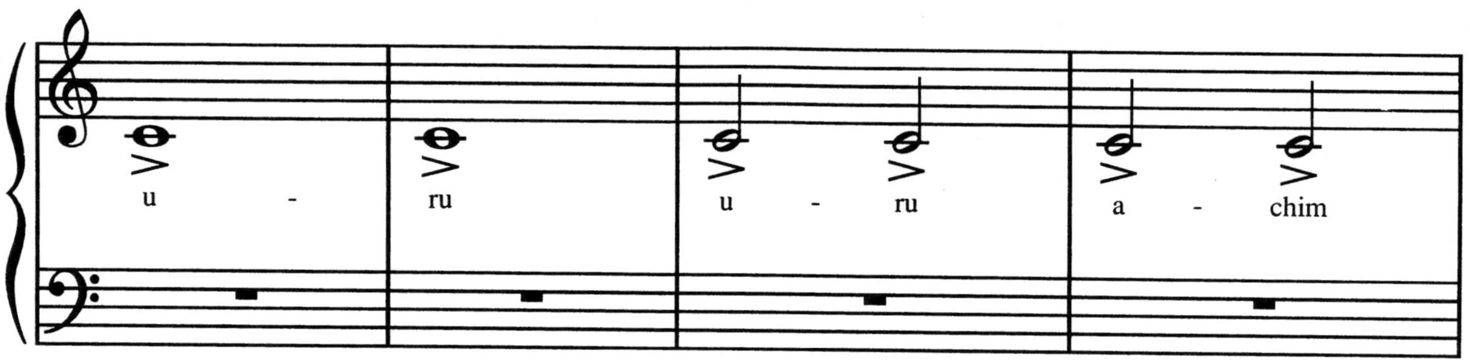
u - ru u - ru a - chim

uru a - chim b' - lev sa - mey - ach uru a - chim b' - lev sa - mey - ach

uru a - chim b' - lev sa - mey - ach uru a - chim b' - lev sa - mey - ach
cresc.

uru a - chim uru a - chim b' - lev sa - mey - ach
f
rit.

TZENA TZENA

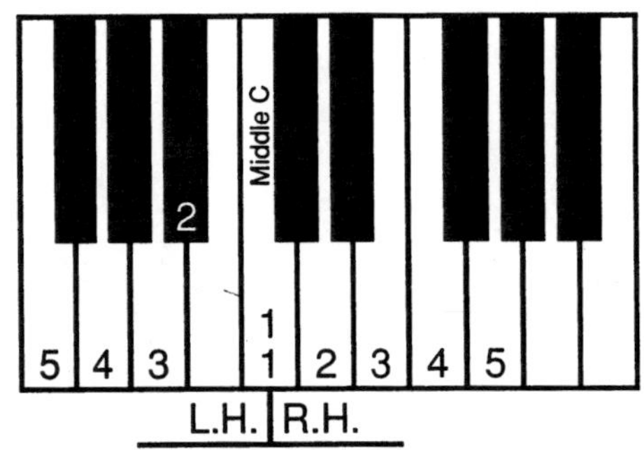
Middle C
2
5 4 3
1
1 2 3 4 5
L.H. R.H.

I. MIRON and J. GROSSMAN
Arranged by ROBERT SCHULTZ

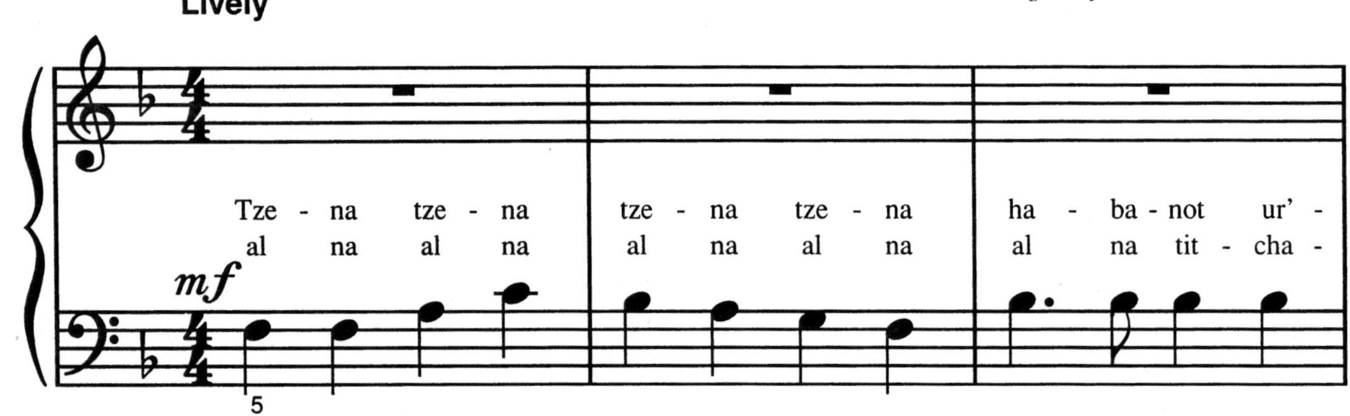
Lively
Tze - na tze - na tze - na tze - na ha - ba - not ur' -
al na al na al na al na al na tit - cha -
mf
5

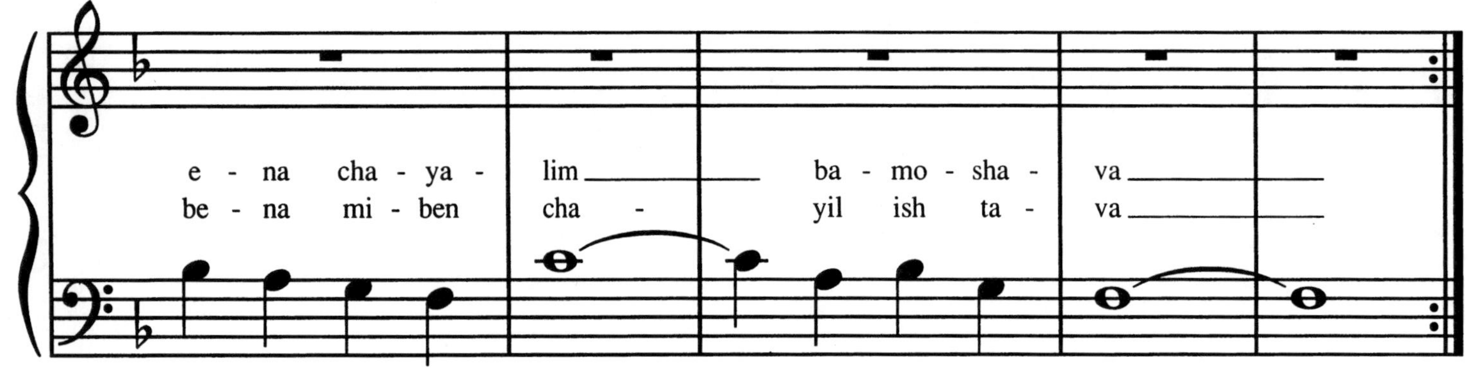
e - na cha - ya - lim ba - mo - sha - va
be - na mi - ben cha - yil ish ta - va

4
tze - na tze - na ha - ba - not ur' - e - na cha - ya -
al na al na al na tit - cha - be - na mi - ben

© 1992 by BEAM ME UP MUSIC, c/o Belwin Mills Publishing Corp. (ASCAP)
All Rights Assigned to and Controlled by Alfred Publishing Co., Inc.
All Rights Reserved including Public Performance. Printed in USA.

1. 2.

lim ba - mo - sha - va
cha - yil ish tza - va

3 4 5 4

tze - na tze - na tze - na tze - na tze - na

tze - na tze - na tze - na tze - na tze - na tze - na

3 4

tze - na tze - na tze - na tze - na tze - na

tze - na tze - na tze - na tze - na tze - na

f

HEVENU SHALOM ALECHEM

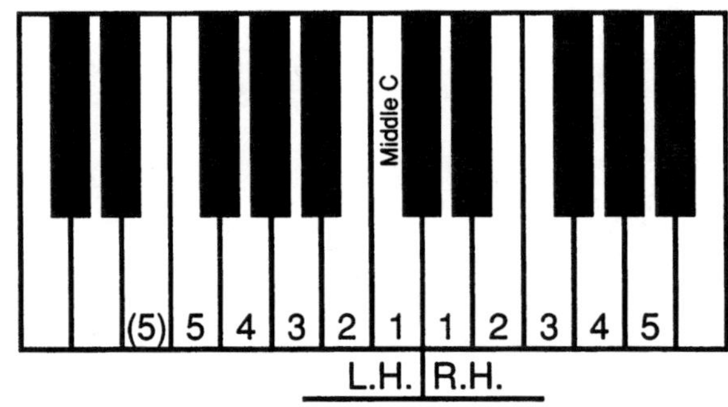
Middle C
(5) 5 4 3 2 1 1 2 3 4 5
L.H. R.H.

TRADITIONAL
Arranged by ROBERT SCHULTZ

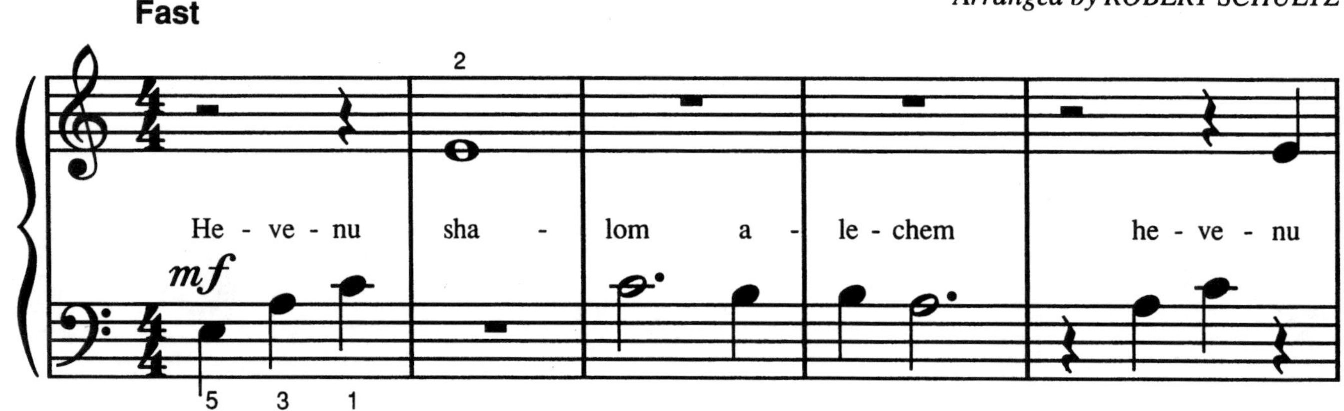
Fast
2
He - ve - nu sha - lom a - le - chem he - ve - nu
mf
5 3 1

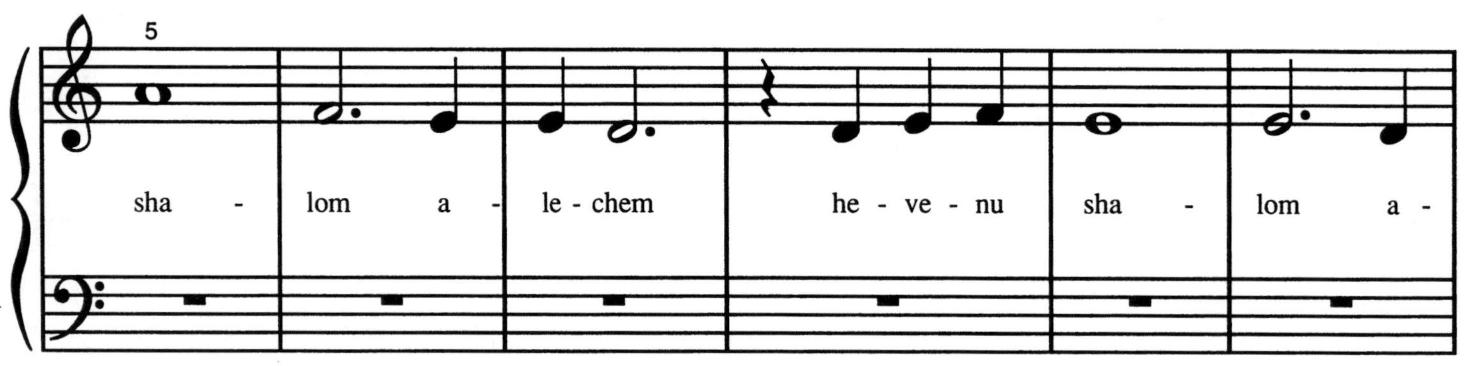
5
sha - lom a - le - chem he - ve - nu sha - lom a -

le - chem he - ve - nu sha - lom sha - lom sha - lom a - le - chem
f

© 1992 by BEAM ME UP MUSIC, c/o Belwin Mills Publishing Corp. (ASCAP)
All Rights Assigned to and Controlled by Alfred Publishing Co., Inc.
All Rights Reserved including Public Performance. Printed in USA.